JON MICHAEL
CHURCH

7/13/1958

7/2/2000

Praise for *Outliving Michael*

One of the responsibilities of spiritual teachers is to remind their friends that EVERYTHING IS IMPERMANENT. And that means we are all going to die! Steven Reigns's gentle reminder of this isn't fraught with images of Ganges burning ghats or Tibetan sky burials. Instead, he leads us through the life, love, and death of his dearest friend in a way that poetically and lovingly prepares us for our own final journey. Isn't that what art does so beautifully? It can give light, peace, and permission to embrace even the Big Endgame Thank you, sweet Steven.

— Linda Montano, *Art in Everyday Life, Performance Artists Talking in the Eighties*

When you know a friend is dying, every moment is enormous. It's all you have. In Outliving Michael, Reigns writes about the enormity of love and loss of a deep friendship. When we're present with one another, we have everything we need. The writing here is so alive. I have great respect for all of Steven Reigns's work, and this is yet another fine example.

— Natalie Goldberg, *Three Simple Lines, Writing on Empty*

A moving elegy for a gay young/beloved/friend and a tribute to his life.

— John Rechy, *City of Night, After the Blue Hour*

Steven Reigns has given me an incredible gift in his stunning elegy, Outliving Michael. (not a gift in the sense of a filmmaker who claimed his new film was a gift; and Steven's friend Michael responded: "I hope he's kept the receipt") This collection of poems is a gift that will stay with me. I am not able to return it; its power has already pierced me. For those of us who have lost people we love—a love that is powered by the lack of love we find in our families—Outliving Michael has renewed my own lost loves with a vividness that makes the past present. Flesh will disintegrate, but wit remains. Lovers will depart, but friendship remains. Of what betrayal can we accuse the beloved who change our deepest sense of self? Of leaving us too soon? Steven Reigns has indeed outlived Michael, but not, in this Funny, elegant requiem, outlived his love for Michael."

— Paula Vogel, *The Baltimore Waltz, Mother Play*

A disarmingly honest portrait in poems that reads like a promise between companions departed, here, and yet to arrive.

— Jeremy Atherton Lin, *Gay Bar, Deep House*

Once I started reading this book, these collections of fragments, I couldn't stop reading. Reigns has built a man from torn scraps of a life, a friendship, a bond. A portrait, a collage, of Michael, of the devastation of AIDS, of aftermath. Love and death, they say, is all you need to make poetry. And memory. I cried, for Michael, for myself, for everyone I have ever loved. You will, too. I promise you.

— Dorianne Laux, *Only As the Day is Long, Life on Earth*

Drag queen by night, travel agent by day, Michael Church of Naples, Florida, died of AIDS in July 2000. He lives in the book of Steven Reigns, first poet laureate of West Hollywood. Outliving Michael is an homage to a flamboyant mentor offering advice about romance in the absence of romance, offering advice about life in the absence of life: "I was the young sapling he nourished/in brief visits and through phone lines,/as decay set in." Aristotle said a friend is another self. Michael Church said: "I have two subjects for you: to write about me, of course, and me!" Me and me along with Plato's Academy, Michael Church gave Steven Reigns another self to distill a queer bravery to build this raw volume about an inscrutable mentor and a boy without support that roars into the present. So long lives this, Michael, and this gives life to thee. Bravo, poet.

— Spencer Reece, *The Clerk's Tale, The Secret Gospel of Mark*

Tender, with encounters of pranks, intimacy, glitter, and drag this magnificent poetic verse is a tribute to the author's beloved eccentric friend, Michael who died of AIDS. The writing walks us through vignettes of desire, passion, dreams and hopes, chosen family, and keen wit all while damning those desperate, traumatic times. Reflecting on life's purpose in surviving,Outliving Michael inspires the reader with the sacred trust and immensity of deep shared friendship. This illuminating collection restores us as a welcoming soliloquy for a generation. While reading I felt restoration and humanity. Reigns's words twinkle with the generosity of his lived experience. A must read.

— Karen Finley, *Shock Treatment, COVID Vortex Anxiety Opera Kitty Kaleidoscope Disco*

"After Michael died," writes Steven Reigns, "most of my recollections/ began with/ After Michael died." That sentence elegantly and painfully describes the after-lives of those of us who lost a beloved companion – a lover, friend, parent, sibling or child to AIDS. And though we're still here, awake to the present, those old griefs are a memory away, and memory, as this collection demonstrates, both wounds and consoles at once.

— Mark Doty, *Deep Lane, My Alexandria*

Outliving Michael

Outliving Michael

by Steven Reigns

MOON
TIDE PRESS

~ 2025 ~

Outliving Michael

Editor-in-chief
Eric Morago

Operations Associate
Shelly Holder

Associate Editors
Mackensi E. Green
Ellen Webre
Allysa Murray

Editor Emeritus
Michael Miller

Front cover art
Cover photograph of Michael Church by Ericson Proper
Cover concept Darin Klein; cover designer Joshua Taylor

Frontispiece concept
Amy Scholder

Book design
Michael Wada

Moon Tide logo design
Abraham Gomez

Outliving Michael
is published by Moon Tide Press

Moon Tide Press
6709 Washington Ave. #9297
Whittier, CA 90608
www.moontidepress.com

FIRST EDITION

Printed in the United States of America

ISBN # 978-1-957799-37-7

Dedicated to Michael Church
(January 13, 1958–July 2, 2000)

I have 2 subjects
for you
to write about
me, of course
and me!

Contents

Death is one moment, and life is so many of them.

— Tennessee Williams,
   The Milk Train Doesn't Stop Here Anymore

His father did the books
for Steve Rubell,
got Michael a job
as a bottle boy at Studio 54.
Michael said, *I probably picked up*
three bottles that entire summer.
He spent most work
hours on the dance floor. I
smile thinking of him
strawberry-haired, sweating, in
a white T-shirt, bar rag in his
low-slung jeans, bottle of poppers
in his pocket as he danced.
AIDS was already in
the room but not in his body,
and no one knew anything anyway.
There was just the dancing, sweating,
sex, drugs, and disco.

He loved Judy, but not that one.
Judge Judy – creator of order,
righter of wrongs, punisher of the guilty.
Michael would lie on the bed all day,
laugh loudly at her quips, recount stories
and scenarios from the day's episode to me.
Judy lived in Naples, and he was always
on the lookout, but it never happened.
Her book was proudly displayed
on his coffee table:
Beauty Fades, Dumb Is Forever.
This was toward the end of his life
when he'd lost weight,
eyes and cheeks sunken,
front teeth jutting over his lips.
He made me schedule doctors' visits
around the show. I caught glimpses
of her show at his house
where he'd indiscriminately rewatch episodes.

The virus had crept in, betrayed his body.
robbed him of his looks,
held hope hostage,
murdered his lover,
absconded with his future.
Did he imagine Judy ruling in his favor,
meting out justice to right all the wrongs?

After Michael died,
most of my recollections
began with
After Michael died.

Sting

I.

I spent my childhood running
away from bees in the backyard.
Feared every sight or mention of them
or the stories of someone dying from a sting.
I, having never been stung,
worried that I might have an allergy.
It was only much later, when I read
about bees dying in droves,
that I was worried about them.
By that time I was a gardener, understood
their purpose and power.

II.

I was picking plums in Natalie's yard,
bees buzzed around my outstretched arm.
I remembered they used to scare me.
The overripe plums would slip off,
and the bees swarmed around each picked plum
We had so much in common, wanting the sugar.

III.

I think back on how scared I was
of being gay, of gay men.
There were, after all, the men who trespassed,
as if my young body was theirs to forage.
I was not ripe or willing, but they took anyway.
Then, when I was 14, in a discount clothing
store, I saw two men with teased hair, cackling
at each other's jokes, hands flitting,
as if they were waving off bees.
I browsed a nearby rack to watch them.
I wanted their confidence, joy, and what I thought
they must do in bed together. I didn't want
to be them at all, yet I knew I was.
I went to bars long before I should have,
a fake ID getting me in the door, and all
the older men swarmed around me.

IV.

Years later, when I met Michael,
he was drunk and in drag, sitting at
the bar of Naples's only gay club.
He tugged on the side of his wig
until it slid off his bald head,
leaving a face full of makeup
and two double pearl drop earrings.
Even intoxicated, his wit was quick.
I'd feel its sting minutes after a comment.
We buzzed around the bar that night –
Vodka the nectar we consumed.
That night, I knew I wanted to spend
every moment I could with him.
I had found my queen.

V.

With Michael, I began to lose
my fear of older men, to let go
of the fright accumulated
from predators of my past
and the media messages about
what they carried and passed
with sexual carelessness.
They had been dying in droves.
Their cum and blood could kill me,
like the sting I'd always feared.

I dated Italo Renault before meeting Michael.
Our passionate affair involved
writing letters, lots of fucking, and only
one argument about trust, that was big enough
to kill the romance, but not friendship.
We talked on the phone,
gave book recommendations.
When he didn't return my call,
I assumed he was busy, then one day
his line was disconnected.
I called the salon where he worked,
and a voice on the other end said Italo
had died and gave me his mother's number.
Renee was as sweet as Italo had always said.
He had been sick and gone to the emergency room.
They sent him home, said the fever would pass.
He died alone in his bed at the age of twenty-six
and was found two days later.
I barely kept my composure on the phone.
And, though he was my best friend,
I never said anything to Michael.
What I wanted to do
was warn him about things
he already knew. That
the virus was a killer, that he should
be cautious, and that the
medical professionals
we wanted to trust,
we shouldn't.

Toward the end, he had trouble sleeping,
would stay up watching television or reading.
I woke up to a note: he had seen two
poets on TV, wanted me to read
their work, told me to look them up.
So much time has passed, I've surpassed
the careers of both of them.
But on the other side of that paper
is something I had forgotten about.
He scrawled that I should write
about him. Finding it in my papers,
all these years later,
was lovely permission.

Michael's lover Ramón cared
for the unfit animals of the world.
He filled his home in Spain with
broken-winged birds, cats with limps,
dogs with mange. Ramón liked to care
for the things others didn't care for.
Michael went back to America,
intending to return to Spain,
but then a tearful phone call came:
Ramón was sick, and Michael must have it too.
A week later, the phone rang again:
Ramón's resentful mother telling Michael
that his lover was dead.

I don't know what Michael did
with his suggestion of a diagnosis,
with his grief over Ramón.
I don't even know how long it was –
weeks, maybe months – when a mutual
friend told him Ramón was still alive
and didn't understand why Michael
never called or came back.
Michael called, and when Ramón's
mother answered, he didn't say hello, just
Put him on the phone – now.
Maybe it was guilt or the tone in his voice,
but she complied.
He told Ramón, who could only reply in whispers,
that he loved him, was coming back to him that night.

Michael was a travel agent in the days before
the internet. I imagine his fingers deftly
making his own reservation in DOS code,
packing bags, flying across the Atlantic,
his boyfriend now Lazarus.
He arrived just in time to sit beside Ramón's bed,
hold his hand, as the man he loved died again.

Michael loved to hear the stories
of whom I was dating or fucking.
He was kind to those he met in person,
even if he didn't like them.
His default mode was storyteller, not listener.
But when he focused his attention on me,
onto any hurt or upset I felt in the rocky
relationships of my youth, his advice
was an un-refracted beam of light.
When Michael gave his attention, he gave
all of it, reserved nothing for anything else.

The last time he visited me, I was dating
an older man – also named Michael – who drove us
in his Infiniti and picked up the check at dinner.
This pleased Michael, who later told me: *Keep him.*
It was a kind of end-of-life matchmaking, a storyline
to take into the brain fog that would envelop him.
Even after I broke off the relationship,
Michael would say he was happy I found someone.
I never corrected him and let him be content
that someone would be there to take care of me
after he was gone.

Star was a massage therapist
who went by the name Gretta.
Fearful her real name might sound solicitous.
She invited a friend to the party.
He was a bitchy queen –
none of us liked him.
He would sneer at comments
and was especially awful to me,
the youngest in the group
and the easiest to pick on.
He disappeared at the party.
We didn't think anything about it,
but then he emerged and soon left.
The bathroom smelled terrible –
around the toilet were the dark
brown marks of diarrhea.
Then I recalled his grabbing his jacket
and putting it around his waist. I didn't like
him yet felt sorry for him.
Looking back now, I can see his weight loss,
his pitted skin, all that hubris to hide HIV,
the lashing out at others, his rage
and fear that the party was nearly over.

Michael told me the story only once
about the time Ramón hit him.
He acted like this was a secret
not to be shared, but I could tell
he'd refined and rehearsed it, so
it wasn't the first or even the fifth time
he'd told the story.
They were in Spain, I can't remember
where, but I imagine it in Ronda,
the cliffside city full of twisting roads.
The two of them left dinner, Michael –
young and upset with Ramón –
driving dangerously, erratically.
Ramón demanded he pull over.
Once outside the convertible,
Ramón promptly hit him.
Then, in a mixture of Spanish
and English, told Michael to stop
with his dramatics.
Michael said the moment changed his life,
slapped him out of childishness.
If anyone had ever told me a lover
would hit me and I'd stay,
I'd think they were crazy.

We shared many meals together
at Pazzo, Sunrise Café. I made him go
to the Flamingo Café because they made
French toast out of croissants.
Michael hated it, left the table early to smoke.
I took him to my favorite thrift store
Hospice Treasures because
they had cheap, organized books.
All the clerks knew me there.
Michael bought a gay novel I can't recall.
He didn't donate to them, would eventually give
all his things to the thrift store named
after his dead best friend, Joe Logsdon.
When he made a purchase, the receipt
would print Joe's name at the top,
a constant reminder of loss
in this place of plenty.

Life is short
Death is long

In the photographs I've been sent,
sometimes I see the Michael I knew,
sometimes the image surprises me,
and sometimes it's not the Michael I knew at all.
And in the images toward the end
I long to sit with him,
hold his thin, freckled hand,
comfort him,
and then tell the story beyond
how he looked at the end.

Caeb and I went to visit Wes
in a Barstow hospital.
Wes stayed there for weeks,
was losing his hair. He was
more Caeb's friend than mine,
but I had the hair clippers.
In hospital room 16A
we both took turns shaving
Wes's head. He cried
and talked of his dead
lover, who had died in a
car accident. He was a veterinarian,
coming back from a home visit.

At age twenty-three,
it was the first time
I heard of a gay man dying
of anything other than AIDS. And here
was Wes, dying of cancer,
alone in a bed. Like so many
of the men I had known
or slept with
or just said hi to at the bar.
So many of them were alone,
hiding out from the disease
or the effects the disease
had on their bodies.

I've outlived so many
of the men in my life.
The most painful has always been,
will always be, outliving Michael.

I was invited down for Christmas,
the third we spent together.
That year, he hosted a dinner with
family and friends.
When walking
from the kitchen to the living room,
Michael plucked the mistletoe off
the ceiling, fashioned it on his belt buckle,
and walked around the party.

The last time he came to visit me
he spent that last night and all of
the next day in bed.
This had become common.
His losing steam. I packed for him and
put the bags in his car. He left,
promised to call when he got home.
After two and a half hours I called, got his voicemail.
His call came two hours later.
He was beaming on the other end.
Driving down I-75, he had been cruised. A man in a blue pickup
had signaled to Michael with his rainbow sticker on his car.
Michael followed him off a ramp,
into an unnamed Florida town, and
they went to the stranger's small apartment
and had sex. Michael said,
With my baseball cap on,
I don't think he realized how old I was.
I didn't ask whether Michael had told him
about his HIV status or if a condom was used.
What I didn't say was how I resented
that Michael could rally for this stranger after
having lain lifeless during his visit with me. The thrill
in his voice kept me from saying anything, and this was
the last time I heard him happy. He was electric,
energized by the attention, the spark of their bodies
against each other. He was,
once again, the object of desire.

Mistletoe hanging above his penis,
Michael was the joke at that Christmas party.
He never told me of the times he was rejected
for his status, but it must have happened.
What was below that mistletoe
back then,
was a dangerous thing.

I read self-help books
then metaphysical, new age books.
I believed in deities, angels
manifesting, and symbols.
Everything was mystically significant.
Every outside action was
caused by inner thoughts.
When my car's rearview mirror fell off
I told Michael maybe it was a sign,
a reminder to stop looking back,
forget what was behind and think of the future.
Michael nodded and smiled:
Maybe you just have a screw loose.

He started losing his thick, red hair;
kept it buzzed short, had taken to
wearing baseball caps,
the free kind with embroidered logos.

His nine-year-old neighbor on the news,
she had a tumor, spent countless nights
in hospital beds, days hooked up
to soul-draining chemo.
Michel couldn't stop talking about her,
horrified she could die so young,
the unspoken truth that he was going
to as well – still too young.
Everything he wanted to say about himself
he said about her: it was unfair, unjust,
senseless, and the slowness cruel.

One night on the way to dinner,
he saw the family pull into their driveway.
He offered neighborly support to the parents.
The girl was shy, bald, with dark-ringed eyes.
Always animated, Michael loved to make
someone laugh, so he pulled off his cap:
Looks like we go to the same barber.
She giggled, they said their goodbyes,
and Michael got into his car and cried.

I'm wearing a necktie on my forehead,
Michael said over the phone.
Like Oliva Newton-John in "Physical,"
I asked, laughing at the thought.
Exactly like her!

There was a new dress code
at the travel agency, requiring
a shirt and tie, but Michael rebelled:
They didn't say where
the tie was to be worn.

I, a notorious rule-follower,
was concerned: *Aren't you afraid*
you'll get fired?

But Michael was confident:
I'm the best agent in here,
they can't get rid of me.

He'd made himself indispensable,
could not be fired no matter how flamboyant he acted.
Gayness was reason enough for termination.
They never would. They need me too much.

I have a photo of Michael,
head cocked, ratty wig
pulled from the trunk of his
car plopped on his head.
His right hand in the air,
as if holding a cigarette.
He was energic, alive, and we
felt like there was nothing but time.
We were in the apartment parking lot
where I lived with my first boyfriend.
We spent the day at an exhibition
of artifacts pulled from the Titanic.
Plates and evening programs
stained by decades in the
dark ocean, used by people
who thought they were unsinkable,
that the party would last forever.

Michael bequeathed his humor to me
via pay phone in the Atlanta airport.
My long-distance romance over,
I was flying back to Florida, single again.
Michael didn't like him anyway.
When I excitedly said he had two cars,
Michael asked, *Why, they're not shoes?*

As Michael heard my disappointment,
I spotted an older man watching me,
rubbing his crotch suggestively.
I whispered the details to Michael, who asked
Well, how is your herpes?
Confused, I blurted out, *My herpes?*
The man heard me and his hand moved
like lightning away from his bulge.
Michael howled with laughter,
fed me line after line of disgusting
and outlandish diseases and situations.
He was a long-distance ventriloquist,
pulling strings through the phone line
giving me his quick wit and cadence.

In his second-to-last year,
Michael had trouble getting hard.
Viagra was a miracle drug
all over the news and late-night
monologues, but his doctor said
he didn't need it or sex
not-so-subtly hinted that Michael
was a danger to others.
I told him I'd ask around,
bought two pills from a fast-talking
drug dealer my friend Eric was dating,
who warned me about side-effects –
upset stomach, abnormal vision –
and to avoid grapefruit.
I paid $40, a stretch for me at the time,
and never asked Michael for the money.
I mailed the pills, enclosed a note:
I want you to be happy,
I want you to fuck your brains out.

Chuck sent me a photo of Michael
in a pool, one hand on the deck,
arms freckling in the bright sun,
he's squinting, grinning, and his other
hand is skimming the water
and pointing to a friend. This is not
the way I remember him.
In the photo, his smile fits his face,
there are no teeth jutting out from
hollowed cheeks under sunken eyes.
I was that age when I thought I knew everything.
Thought Michael's aging was just life, not AIDS.
One day he called to tell me a story
about trying on jeans at the mall:
The 32s and 31s were way too loose,
he said with excitement.
I'm wearing a 30. I love AIDS.
We laughed a long time, me oblivious
to the clock running down
and he deflecting fear.
Every shirt tucked into dress pants or 501s
to show off his slim waist, getting slimmer,
was cause for celebration.
We were young, tough, defiant, laughing
in the face of death that was laughing back at us.

Michael Ranucci saw a therapist for years,
exploring his past lives.
I can't recall how many he had,
but there was always a flair for the exotic.
While I knew him,
to live up to his former selves and
prepare for the next adventure,
he got a trainer, went to the gym
daily, became buff, no hint
of his former scrawny self.
It was as if while I knew him,
he had lived two lives already.
Heather had trouble differentiating
the Michaels in my life, called this one
Past Life Regression Michael.
We lost touch before my Michael died.
I would have loved his reassurance
that our paths would cross again someday –
I'd see him in this life and the next.

After Michael's death, I rushed
into a relationship thinking I would avoid grief.
Then, back in Florida, a whirlwind of odd jobs:
doorman, bartender, underwear model.
While getting an HIV test, I decided to volunteer.
The organization's demographic was black gay men,
which must have made my white face a surprise.
I worked with high-risk youth, didn't mince words
or shame, used matter-of-fact messaging.
I told hundreds they were HIV-positive.
It was hard. The pain was terrible.
It was as if my life became consumed with HIV.
Friends were worried about me at my job
and how it devoured my life.
I assured them I was fine, that
similar to the Florida hurricanes I had lived through
the calm was being in the center

I knew Blanche before I ever met Michael.
His drag alter-ego was notorious in Naples.
While the other queens were serving showgirl,
songstress, or streetwalker, Blanche strolled
in from the pages of *Town and Country*, a lady
of impeccable means, with delicate earrings,
gold bracelets, a clutch. Serving realness.
Michael lived for drag, a connoisseur of
crass and camp, how to subvert and offend
with a look, a gesture, a song.
Everyone called him Blanche, but I called him
Michael, and he allowed it. Maybe as a reminder,
a tether to reality, a portal back home.

We set a blanket out for fireworks
at the park, a plaid of black and brown.
Michael packed a picnic basket.
A couple sat beside us,
blankets almost touching.
They were on a date. We were not.
She was a doctor and he in business.
I had spent most of the day alone,
was in a sour mood, sat withdrawn,
watched as a conversation ensued.
The couple engaged with Michael.
The sky lit up, and I witnessed again
how easily he could talk with anyone.
A week earlier we had been in a bar
sharing drinks with a hustler, days
before it was with ingenue Carla,
and now this couple. Their
attention to each other
dimmed. Everyone wanted
Michael's light to
shine on them.

I wasn't drunk, just desirous
of the dark-haired photographer
with big eyes and romantic accent.
We fucked without abandon
and regrettably without a
condom. It wasn't a death drive
but rather a zest to live and maybe a way
to share more with Michael, but I
did not want to die like him.

The next day I made calls to my doctor,
the GMHC, and AIDS hotline. Asked
about what I had read about
post-exposure prophylaxis,
the treatment for needlesticks
and condom breaks. I hadn't
had an accident but a judgment lapse and hoped
they'd still help me. The treatment
so new, my doctor knew nothing, and my
other calls got transferred from staff to staff.
I was told I had less than twenty-four hours
from exposure to take it.
Found out the medication and dosage, called
my doctor, begged for the script, rushed
to the pharmacy across town that had HIV meds,
waited in a long line.

When I think of myself
at twenty-six, that's what I see:
cordless phone in my hand
while I dialed for my life to live.

Daisy was the name he gave his white poodle,
after *The Great Gatsby* but I never recall him
talking about F. Scott, only Andrew Holleran.
He touted Holleran and Judge Judy, held space
for both. His friends were a similar mix.
So was his clothing, a mix of Saks and thrift.
We ate at restaurants on Fifth Avenue and at Perkins.
He'd serve elaborate meals on trivets
he made from Continental Baths tiles.
Michael had feet in both worlds, yet now
he's not in any world except my memories
and this writing – that is neither
Holleran nor Sheindlin – but the compulsion
to write about him, honor him, memorialize him
is the only way I can give back an ounce
of what he gave to me.

My mother tells me that
before their Christmas dinner
they all toasted me.
Glasses held by the same
hands that hit me as a child,
clinking above the oak table.
Saying my name, honoring me,
wishing I were there.
I was with Michael,
sitting on his overstaffed sofa
listening to the drag queen CD
God Shave the Queen.
We laughed, carried on,
both of us in loungewear.
Michael told stories of his past
or mimicked the performers.
He felt like my true family
and all the family I needed.

I was to be on
the cover of a magazine,
and the editor emailed questions.
When Michael called,
I read him my replies.
He was quiet and then
told me to answer more thoughtfully:
Respond as if your soulmate will read it.

I scrapped every word.
I wrote as if my answers
were a beacon and that
magazine the lighthouse.
I called Michael the next day,
read him my new answers,
and I could feel his smile through the phone.
There you go.

I still take his advice,
think of that unknown, unnamed man
I'm to love forever, who would love me forever.
Sometimes I think of Michael
as my perfect audience, ear pressed to the receiver,
waiting to hear every word, believing greatness was in me.
And if my words met his expectations for me,
he would reply
There you go.

He had a large stack of the memorial cards handed at funerals,
friends and lovers stolen by AIDS.
I had joked once
that he might need a recipe box
to categorize or alphabetize the mounting stack.

He thought for a moment, said
They are organized by course.
I'll have to make decisions!

So he began to shout out the
long list of names and where he would place them:

Jose – entrée
Michael – hors d'oeuvre
Susan – hors d'oeuvre
Joey – entrée
Jonathan – hors d'oeuvre
Alex – hors d'oeuvre
and for his last lover
Ramón – dessert

As a travel agent, Michael
memorized every airport's code.
I think of him every time I book
a flight online, his job a relic,
entering codes for DEN, TPA, LGA, STL.
He booked a flight for me to LHR once,
my first transatlantic trip,
told me the best time to fly, what to eat,
what to see, and did it all on discounts
and insider fares for his penniless friend.
Once I was on board, sitting next to the
emergency door, the stewardess asked
if I'd be willing to open it in case of emergency.
I said yes, appreciated the extra legroom.
She smiled, winked, and said,
Someone knew what they were doing
when they booked the flight.

I had ten minutes to spare and thought
I'll come out to my parents,
as if it were a neglected task on my to-do list.
Dialed my childhood home, told my mother straightforwardly.
She cried, asked if that was why I had long hair.
Later that night, on the lanai furniture
Joey bought on credit knowing he'd die soon,
then willed to Michael, I told him what I had done.
He sat and smoked Parliaments as I told him
of my effortlessness. I grew up being told
I was a disappointment, felt unloved,
unwanted, and their cruelness gave adult me
a gift, I never feared
losing something
I never had.

I cried in the car driving down the 101,
tuned into some NPR show about trees
and how it takes decades for them to die.
All the while, sending underground signals
of change and danger, nutrients to those
in need.

Michael's death seemed like this –
a slow, drawn-out withering away.
But decades on, I see now he went so fast,
and I was the young sapling he nourished
in brief visits and through phone lines,
as decay set in.

I was in the Berkshires, shacked up with a lover,
when I got the news. Retrieved a message left by his mother
on my answering machine at home.
One of my best friends was dead, and although
I expected the news, I didn't know how to grieve him.
Michael had grown up there, so I drove around town
aimlessly, until I saw a craft shop with his name, Michaels.
I walked in and bought twelve large packages
of costume crystals that glimmered even in
the yellow fluorescent lights.
I drove with them nestled in the passenger seat,
treated them as if they were actual jewels,
as if they had value, as if they were Michael.
I stopped at the edge of the Housatonic River
walked across the bridge in the summer night,
and pulled the first package from my pocket.
The crystals glittered in oncoming headlights
and then as they spun and tumbled into the water.
I did this eleven more times, crystals and tears
falling from the bridge.
I wasn't religious, but as I opened the last package
I remembered *The Tibetan Book of the Dead*
instructing to tell the ones we've lost
that it's ok to go. *I release you*, I said, as the last
crystal shimmered and disappeared into the water.

On the elliptical trainer
I'd flip through magazines
looking for the memorials.
To read about the lives of others,
marvel at the accomplishment,
what one can do in a lifetime.
It'd motivate me to push harder
to stay longer on the machine.
Every thrust of my thigh
every foot pedal down,
was my wanting to live
to become one of them.

While Michel's life was ending,
I was busy toppling mine:
quit a good job, got caught up
in a long-distance affair, worked retail.
I was packing for another trip
when the phone rang. It was Michael,
his voice hushed and jumbled from dementia,
words buzzing softly from one disconnected
thought to the next.
I just stayed on the line,
responded when I could, and then,
he said clearly
I want to thank you for everything.
Michael had called for a final goodbye.
He wouldn't have understood then that it was I
who wanted to thank him. For his guidance,
encouragement, the lessening of fear
because of him, I felt less alone.

I thought of you, kicking off your loafers
after work, nodding off on the A train,
waking up to find an unhoused man
putting your shoes into a black garbage bag.
You stood up in your nylon socks,
grabbed your shoes from his bag, said
You can't go around stealing people's shoes.

I remembered this story
when sitting on a store bench,
lacing up a boot. Did the math,
calculated I was the age you were when you died.
I didn't think you'd die. Didn't think, for some
reason, I'd ever be as old as you had been.
Sitting there in an ill-fitting boot, I realized
my life blueprint was gone.

Driving through Arizona
there's a highway sign
announcing the Dead River.

I kept thinking about it for miles.
To name something for what it used to be.
And I thought of Michael and the river
where I threw jewels for him and who
downstream might have found them.
A terrible fool's gold.

But out in the arid West,
I drive over a bridge of nothing.
Was it ever alive, flowing?
Did it ever take anything
in its current to the ocean?

At the end of 2000
I read singer Kirsty MacColl died,
was hit by a boat while
swimming with her children.
I cried, talked about her to anyone who'd listen.
I sat teary-eyed across from my therapist.
He asked if it was misplaced concerns
about the new year.
Only now, all these years later,
I realize it was about Michael.

The newspaper says tornadoes are
in Texas. I read *tomatoes*,
thus have a hard time
understanding the context
and concern. This keeps
happening. I hold restaurant menus
up to the tea candle on the table,
end sentences with commas.
The young optometrist
tells me it is expected at
my age. I want to tell her
that I'm not old. I've almost
doubled Italo's life. I'm the
same age of Michael
when he died. The day he
passed I kept crying,
thinking how young he was.
I might have forgotten,
had it not been for a photo
of him in a shirt I gave him
the last year of his life,
that he was wearing glasses.

It's said the last thing our parents teach us is how to die.
I learned this from Michael.

There's a fable
of a traveler coming into
a poor, hungry village.
Says he can make stone soup:
starts with a rock and caldron of water
over fire. Sips it, said it needed
a carrot, and someone gives him one,
does the same thing with
onions, peas, and meat.
It's a story about a trickster but
also of gathering resources.

Over the years, I have reached out to many
to discuss Michael – Clay, Chuck,
Beverly, Michael, Ray,
John, Jasper, Juliette, Kim, Ericson, and Christopher.
It was as if the photos they might give me, the stories
they might tell, could create him again for me.
That for one moment
I wouldn't feel hunger.

Michael gave me a copy of
Dancer from the Dance,
told me it was his memoir.
I held the book and laughed.
This is a novel by Andrew Holleran.
But he said it was the closest
thing to his own life that he'd read.
When *The Beauty of Men* came out,
Michael bought it at the mall,
and it sat on his nightstand for years.
The jacket cover's colors matched
his decor, and, knowing Michael, this was
why it stayed there.
The last Holleran book Michael read was
In September, the Light Changes.
The glossy paperback had a railing
overlooking the ocean, blue sky,
and a ghostlike figure looking out to the water.
I didn't read it then, though I could have
when I sat on his couch in those months I
stayed in Naples to be with him,
on those long afternoons he spent in bed
sleeping or watching TV with the dog by his side.

His dementia frustrated him so much
he threw his cordless phone on the lawn.
Those last few months were terrible.
I tried to take care of him and couldn't.
Our May-September friendship
didn't allow a restructure. He wasn't so accepting
and I, so young, wasn't a good caregiver.

He painted his living room salmon
because it went from bright in daylight
to a soft warm in the evening.
When Michael died, the light
changed for me. His walls lustered a little less.
My life did too.
Six years after Michael's death,
I held Holleran's latest book in my hand,
the title still, even all those years later,
aptly fitting: *Grief.*

I could tell from our conversations
Michael's mind was slipping.
Before our Sunday morning call
I hooked up a recording device
bought at Radio Shack.
I wanted to preserve as much
of Michael as I could.
I've only listened to the tape once.
Besides its high-pitched squeal
are my nervous laughter, forced
good cheer, inane comments.
I fear I wasn't giving a scared, dying man
what he needed. There were so many
things I wanted to say but didn't know how.
When my grandmother was dying,
I walked into her hospice room
and shared my memories,
of how I felt loved by her, how
she made me laugh,
that my life was better because of her.
That I would miss her and that in big moments
of my life I would think of her. I told her
everything I wished I'd said to Michael.

When Michael took me to the exhibition
of artifacts looted from the Titanic,
we stood in a long line to look
at dinnerware, dresses, and deck chairs
dredged from the icy Atlantic.
I became bored and restless as Michael
stood silently, captivated by this treasure
I thought was drippy debris.
But that is what I'm doing to him now,
diving and forging into the past,
trying to bring every scrap of Michael
back to the surface.
In some way, trying to make him real again,
with his tight 501s and bronzered face,
the tasteful tasseled drapes in the living room
he painted salmon.

I don't know what to do with all these memories
except display them like an exhibition.
Here is a man who meant something to me
and who could mean something to you.
Here is a man who lived a large life cut short.
Line up, view every shard and scrap, hold him
in value like I do. Then step this way,
because the museum is vast
in its hurt and memories. Here is Italo, Peter, Timothy,
Jeffery, Joey, and so many more.
The line to see the ones we loved is long.

There's a famous restaurant in New York,
One If by Land, Two If by Sea,
named after Paul Revere's warning
about enemy British troops on the move.
A dead man's favorite place to eat.
Twenty years ago, Michael said,
I have to take you there.
I said, *I'd love that,*
and I would have but, I didn't believe
it would happen, and, looking back,
he too knew it wouldn't.

A year after his death, I was in New York
but didn't go. I didn't want to sit at a table
eating food he could no longer enjoy.
Toward the end, Michael lost his appetite
while he fought to get on disability.
When he got the money, he took
Chuck to Vegas for one last trip.
I remember wishing it was me.
Wanting that time with him,
to sit and eat, talk and laugh
without fear of invasion.

Last night I dreamt we were driving
in my Jeep, singing along to Pet Shop Boys
on the radio, carrying on as if you
were still alive.
Pulling into a parking lot
there was a car that looked just like
the first one I'd ever owned.
That's the model of my first car! I said.
I know, you said with a smile.
I broke down crying, and you disappeared.
You knew my first car and my second.
By the third, you were gone.

Start listening to Piaf
was his advice when I
was struggling with French.
I bought *The Voice of the Sparrow*
at a thrift store,
thought Piaf's emoting
would provide me an
understanding, an intuitive translation.
In one song, I thought
she sang about washing her hair –
cheveux – and then questioned whether it was
about a horse – *cheval*.
When I drove to Parliament House
Michael told me to buy a ticket
to see Miss P perform.
I wanted a night on the dance floor
or fucking in one of the rooms
but followed his suggestion.
She was wicked and crusty
but with kind eyes, pulled
her wig off a smooth bald head
with a grand sweep of her hand.
I knew she had inspired Michael.
I wasn't mastering French
or getting laid, but I was receiving
an education in the avant-garde.
And Michael, my gentle
dutiful *professeur*.

I cut my trip short, left his house early.
Michael's bed was made,
and he was dressed and lying
on top of the ornate sheets.
I can't remember if it was a four-poster,
but I remember it as being big.
Daisy, his white dog, was by his side,
as Michael flipped the channels,
from shows I didn't want to watch.
I kept suggesting things, young
and anxious and wanting
to pack my life with adventure.
I remember the tension between us
late that Sunday morning,
how I would soon pack my bags.
Not recognizing the rest he wanted,
how Michael packed his condo
with everything he loved and
how the outside world wasn't curated.

I step out of bed
feel lower back pain,
feet sore from walking the cobblestone
streets of Paris. This is another trip
I've taken without his
booking my flights
or telling me to grab a pen
as he spelled out what to see.
I wonder what he might have suggested
and realized this morning's pain
is something he had never felt.
My body is older than his ever was, aging
and aching in ways he never experienced.
Those last few years he worried about his health,
upcoming death, the cordless phone he couldn't use, and
how technology was moving beyond him.
I navigated the streets of Paris with my iPhone.

I went to visit him three months before he died.
His kitchen table was littered with photos
and a stack of white legal envelopes.
His cursive script spelled the names
of family and friends on each one.
Michael was distributing not images of himself or his life
but rather of the people in his life back to themselves.
When I left, he handed me an envelope of photos
he had taken or I had mailed to him.
I regret not asking for photos of him. That
was more interesting. Two decades
have passed. I now have a record,
labeled in his handwriting,
I know how Michael saw me.

The Stories of a Life

I

Michael once accused me of doing
my hair with a blender.

II

He was upset with his dog,
Daisy, for pissing in the walk-in closet.
But the soaked carpet made him realize
it was his own, drunk from the night before.

III

Michael took me to his friend's birthday party,
brought a very fancy lamp.
Right before we walked up to the door he said
oh, I'm going to have to put this lampshade on my head
– and that is how he rang the doorbell.

IV

Five nights after a plane crash,
a drag queen with a plastic airplane
on her head threw paper airplanes
into the audience while lip-synching
John Denver's "Leaving on a Jet Plane."
Michael tipped her $50.

V

Michael told me my dancing
reminded him of Elaine from Seinfeld.

VI

Michael roasted lamb to celebrate
my associate degree.
He told me that with my degree
and a dollar and a quarter I could get a cup of coffee.

VII

I drank only White Russians
with Michael, his drink of choice,
and haven't had one since.

VIII

Once in the Galley parking lot,
Michael narrated a drunk man's
bumbling as if he were Howard Cosell
describing every misstep and stumble
until the man fell into the bushes.
We laughed until the medics came.

IX

When my five-year relationship ended,
Michael thought he'd never hear
the end of it and praised me for only
mentioning it three times.

X

Cool Joe's Barbershop advertised
$5 haircuts. Weeks later, a salon across
the street put up a sandwich board:
"We fix $5 haircuts." Michael had to pull
his car over from laughing so hard.

XI

On Thanksgiving,
Michael left a message on
my answering machine that was
just him gobbling.

XII

On July 4,
Michael shouted a message on
my answering machine:
Happy Codependence Day!

XIII

Michael had a side table filled with photos
of his friends who had died. He called it
the dead table. When I arrived
late to his house once, I found he'd put my photo on it.

XIV

When a pretentious filmmaker said his movie
was his gift to the world, Michael said
I really hope he kept the receipt.

XV

He told me in each relationship
there is one person
who loves the other more.
In the best of relationships,
each person believes they are that person.

XVI

Michael's days totaled 15,532.

XVII

Michael handed me a copy
of *Dancer from the Dance*,
said, *It's my life, read it.*
When I gave it back to him
a few days later, I said
He dies in the end.
Michael said, *It's my life.*

La Fin

About the Author

Photo by Evans Vestal Ward

Steven Reigns is a Los Angeles poet and educator and was appointed the first Poet Laureate of West Hollywood. Alongside over a dozen chapbooks, he has published the collections *Inheritance* and *Your Dead Body Is My Welcome Mat*. His collection *A Quilt for David* was published by City Lights and is the product of over ten years of research regarding dentist David Acer's life. Reigns holds a BA in Creative Writing from the University of South Florida and a Master's in Clinical Psychology from Antioch University, and he is a nineteen-time recipient of the Los Angeles County's Department of Cultural Affairs' Artist in Residency Grant. He edited *My Life Is Poetry*, showcasing his students' work from the first-ever autobiographical poetry workshop for LGBT seniors. Reigns has lectured and taught writing workshops around the country to LGBT youth and people living with HIV. Currently he is touring The Gay Rub, an exhibition of rubbings from LGBT landmarks, and is the board president of the Anaïs Nin Foundation. For more information: www.stevenreigns.com.

Publication Credits

Cover photograph of Michael Church by Ericson Proper, Naples, Florida, circa 1992, courtesy of Ericson Proper.

The frontispiece image is a rubbing of Michael Church's grave marker in Naples, Florida, and is part of Steven Reigns's *The Gay Rub*, an exhibition of rubbings from LGBTQ landmarks around the world. Rubbing created by Karen Coors.

Intro image ("I have 2 subjects for you"): note by Michael Church to Steven Reigns, June 2000.

"He had a large stack of the memorial cards handed at funerals" Originally published as "Recipe Box" in *Inheritance*, Sibling Rivalry Press, 2011.

Poem was also included in the feature film *Guys Reading Poems* (dir: Hunter Lee Hughes).

Several of the poems in this publication were written with support from grant awards provided by the City of Los Angeles, Department of Cultural Affairs (DCA). In particular the COLA (City of LA) Independent Master Artist Project grant gave me an artist's stipend to focus on conceptualizing this work.

Completion of this work was supported in part by an arts grant from the City of West Hollywood.

Acknowledgements

Thank you to those who were friends back then, when we shared drinks at The Galley, smoked cigarettes from its vending machine, tipped Blanche and Deliah on stage, laughed at Michael's quips, and now, all these years later, still share stories about him: Jasper Sage, Kimberly Dupuis, Clayton Brown, Ray McCart, Michael Ranucci, Juliette Aiyana, John Walsh III, Christopher Honey, Caeb Colravy, and especially to those who sent me photos: Chuck Kerridge, Ericson Proper, and Beverly Boyne. Michael was big enough for all of us to write our own recollections. This book is just my version, and your kindness and contributions have meant the world.

Darin Klein's friendship has been a grounding force in my Los Angeles life. I've sought his guidance on everything from creative decisions to everyday dilemmas, always trusting his clarity, kindness, cocktails, and deep well of wisdom.

Collin Kelley is the person I turn to with poetry problems and literary community questions. His insight and humor are sharp, his feedback kind, and our shared love of pop and alternative culture makes every conversation a joy.

To my writer friends, who gave great modeling, encouraging words, and enrich my life: David K. Johnson, Julie E. Bloemeke, Bill Addison, Brian Sonia-Wallce, Jen Cheng, David Roman, Kim Dower, Bernard Cooper, Jim Gladstone, Karina Wilson, Francesca Lia Block, the writing accountability group, Ian MacKinnon, Tim Miller, Mariano Zaro, Lois P. Jones, Corey Roskin, John Morgan Wilson, K.M. Soehnlein, Elena Secota, Hunter Lee Hughes, Chris Corkum, and Clement Goldberg. During the shaping of this material, David Trinidad's input, careful edits, and discovery of the title within one of my own poems was an invaluable help.

Thanks to the hospitable friends who may not have named their guest room "Steven's Room" like Michael did, but who've hosted me on visits or let me use their home as a writer's retreat. So many poems were written at other people's dining room tables: Stephanie Recht & Ed Rook, Ann Magnuson & John Betrum, The Cramer Family, Natalie Goldberg, and Mick Cullough & Marybeth Herbener

To my friends who gave support as I talked through challenges and issues with this material: Stephanie Recht, Jenny Waters, and Amy Scholder.

To the many friends who've supported my life and work in more ways than I can count—you know who you are. I'm especially grateful to: BJ Millan, Jonny McGovern, Michael S Kelley, Lisa Kereszi, Brian DeShazor, Martha Roper, Brian Heinberg, Brett Freedman, Shannon Headley, Dano Gregori, Carmelita Nunez, Stacie Strautkalns, Shirley Taylor, Patricia Walters, Clement Leonardo, Karen Coors, Josh Taylor, Evans Vestal Ward, Bradley Betschen, Thaddeus Root, Desmond Clark, The Golden Girls, Alan Joseph Marx, Kris Anthony Guerra, Wayne Stodghill, Tom Lockridge, Frank Zito, Alex Bazley, Eddie Hibbs, and Layla Ross.

Much gratitude to Eric Morago for inviting me into the Moon Tide Press family and for bringing this dear book into the world with such care and consideration.

Also by Steven Reigns

Collections

Outliving Michael
A Quilt for David
Inheritance
My Life is Poetry, preface by Dorothy Allison
Your Dead Body is My Welcome Mat

Chapbooks

For the Love of Peter Hujar
3-Pack Jack
Stu, photos by Lisa Kereszi
As If Memories Were Not Enough
In The Room
Cartography
Ignited

Also Available from Moon Tide Press

Prayers With a Side of Cash, Kathleen Florence (2025)
Somewhere, a Playground, Rich Ferguson (2025)
The Tautology of Water, Giovanni Boskovich (2025)
Take Care, Mark Danowsky (2025)
Dilapitatia, Kelly Gray (2025)
Reluctant Prophets, J.D. Isip (2025)
Enormous Blue Umbrella, Donna Hilbert (2025)
Sky Leaning Toward Winter, Terri Niccum (2024)
Living the Sundown: A Caregiving Memoir, G. Murray Thomas (2024)
Figure Study, Kathryn de Lancellotti (2024)
Suffer for This: Love, Sex, Marriage, & Rock 'N' Roll,
    Victor D. Infante (2024)
What Blooms in the Dark, Emily J. Mundy (2024)
Fable, Bryn Wickerd (2024)
Diamond Bars 2, David A. Romero (2024)
Safe Handling, Rebecca Evans (2024)
More Jerkumstances: New & Selected Poems, Barbara Eknoian (2024)
Dissection Day, Ally McGregor (2023)
He's a Color Until He's Not, Christian Hanz Lozada (2023)
The Language of Fractions, Nicelle Davis (2023)
Paradise Anonymous, Oriana Ivy (2023)
Now You Are a Missing Person, Susan Hayden (2023)
Maze Mouth, Brian Sonia-Wallace (2023)
Tangled by Blood, Rebecca Evans (2023)
Another Way of Loving Death, Jeremy Ra (2023)
Kissing the Wound, J.D. Isip (2023)
Feed It to the River, Terhi K. Cherry (2022)
*Beat Not Beat: An Anthology of California Poets Screwing
    on the Beat and Post-Beat Tradition* (2022)
*When There Are Nine: Poems Celebrating the Life and Achievements
    of Ruth Bader Ginsburg* (2022)
The Knife Thrower's Daughter, Terri Niccum (2022)
2 Revere Place, Aruni Wijesinghe (2022)
Here Go the Knives, Kelsey Bryan-Zwick (2022)
Trumpets in the Sky, Jerry Garcia (2022)
Threnody, Donna Hilbert (2022)

A Burning Lake of Paper Suns, Ellen Webre (2021)
Instructions for an Animal Body, Kelly Gray (2021)
Head *V* Heart: New & Selected Poems, Rob Sturma (2021)
*Sh!t Men Say to Me: A Poetry Anthology in Response
   to Toxic Masculinity* (2021)
Flower Grand First, Gustavo Hernandez (2021)
Everything is Radiant Between the Hates, Rich Ferguson (2020)
When the Pain Starts: Poetry as Sequential Art, Alan Passman
(2020)
This Place Could Be Haunted If I Didn't Believe in Love,
   Lincoln McElwee (2020)
Impossible Thirst, Kathryn de Lancellotti (2020)
Lullabies for End Times, Jennifer Bradpiece (2020)
Crabgrass World, Robin Axworthy (2020)
Contortionist Tongue, Dania Ayah Alkhouli (2020)
The only thing that makes sense is to grow, Scott Ferry (2020)
Dead Letter Box, Terri Niccum (2019)
Tea and Subtitles: Selected Poems 1999-2019, Michael Miller (2019)
At the Table of the Unknown, Alexandra Umlas (2019)
The Book of Rabbits, Vince Trimboli (2019)
Everything I Write Is a Love Song to the World,
   David McIntire (2019)
Letters to the Leader, HanaLena Fennel (2019)
Darwin's Garden, Lee Rossi (2019)
Dark Ink: A Poetry Anthology Inspired by Horror (2018)
Drop and Dazzle, Peggy Dobreer (2018)
Junkie Wife, Alexis Rhone Fancher (2018)
The Moon, My Lover, My Mother, & the Dog,
   Daniel McGinn (2018)
Lullaby of Teeth: An Anthology of Southern California Poetry (2017)
Angels in Seven, Michael Miller (2016)
A Likely Story, Robbi Nester (2014)
Embers on the Stairs, Ruth Bavetta (2014)
The Green of Sunset, John Brantingham (2013)
The Savagery of Bone, Timothy Matthew Perez (2013)
The Silence of Doorways, Sharon Venezio (2013)
Cosmos: An Anthology of Southern California Poetry (2012)
Straws and Shadows, Irena Praitis (2012)
In the Lake of Your Bones, Peggy Dobreer (2012)

I Was Building Up to Something, Susan Davis (2011)
Hopeless Cases, Michael Kramer (2011)
One World, Gail Newman (2011)
What We Ache For, Eric Morago (2010)
Now and Then, Lee Mallory (2009)
Pop Art: An Anthology of Southern California Poetry (2009)
In the Heaven of Never Before, Carine Topal (2008)
A Wild Region, Kate Buckley (2008)
Carving in Bone: An Anthology of Orange County Poetry (2007)
Kindness from a Dark God, Ben Trigg (2007)
A Thin Strand of Lights, Ricki Mandeville (2006)
Sleepyhead Assassins, Mindy Nettifee (2006)
Tide Pools: An Anthology of Orange County Poetry (2006)
Lost American Nights: Lyrics & Poems, Michael Ubaldini (2006)

Patrons

Moon Tide Press would like to thank the following people for their support in helping publish the finest poetry from the Southern California region. To sign up as a patron, visit www.moontidepress. com or send an email to publisher@moontidepress.com.

Anonymous
Robin Axworthy
Conner Brenner
Nicole Connolly
Bill Cushing
Susan Davis
Kristen Baum DeBeasi
Peggy Dobreer
Kate Gale
Dennis Gowans
Alexis Rhone Fancher
HanaLena Fennel
Half Off Books & Brad T. Cox
Donna Hilbert
Jim & Vicky Hoggatt
Michael Kramer
Ron Koertge & Bianca Richards
Gary Jacobelly
Ray & Christi Lacoste

Jeffery Lewis
Zachary & Tammy Locklin
Lincoln McElwee
David McIntire
José Enrique Medina
Michael Miller & Rachanee Srisavasdi
Michelle & Robert Miller
Ronny & Richard Morago
Terri Niccum
Andrew November
Jeremy Ra
Luke & Mia Salazar
Jennifer Smith
Roger Sponder
Andrew Turner
Rex Wilder
Mariano Zaro
Wes Bryan Zwick

JON MICHAEL
CHURCH

7/13/1958
7/2/2000

www.ingramcontent.com/pod-product-compliance
Lightning Source LLC
Chambersburg PA
CBHW031146090426

42738CB00008B/1242